I've Seen Too Much!

By Bishop Dr. Paul Kammer

Copyright Page

ENDORSEMENT

Bishop Paul Kammer: What do I know about him? First, he is a student of the Word of God receiving degrees from the International Miracle Institute and IMI School of Ministry, Pensacola, Florida.

Second, he is a prayer warrior, seeking the face of God for lost souls. I first met Brother Paul in about 2012 when we visited his church in Port Orange, Florida, and the thing I remember most was the presence of the Holy Spirit as you walked through the door. Paul has a great love for the people. In talking with him I learned that he has a great missionary desire as well. In his travels, which include Peru and Columbia, with many miracles taking place, God confirming His Word. In reading an excerpt from his book called: **I've Seen Too Much**, Chapter 4: In Christ We Have Victory; you will see his burning desire for souls.

Bishop William T. White

**Edgewater Church of God
201 S. Ridgewood Ave.
Suite #9
Edgewater, Florida 32132**

FOREWORD

I title this *"I've Seen Too Much,"* because this is a book about faith. The more you see the more you expect of God. The funny thing is the more you see the more you believe. In chapter 2 we are taught to see the way it is in heaven is the way we should live here on earth. God has many promises in His Word that should change the way of life here on earth for us. We are citizens of heaven, we are here as Ambassadors, from Heaven and we have special rights as Heaven's Ambassadors.

Then in chapter 3 we will see that we have nothing to worry about because God started our lives and laid them out before we were even conceived. In fact, you will see that God finished our lives even before it began. All we need to do is believe and follow the Holy Spirit as He leads us.

Then the next chapter shows us that we walk in victory, even before we start. There will be challenges along the way, even hard battles, but as you will see we already have the victory. We will see spiritual doors that God will put before us, and show us the keys that will unlock them and walk through them.

While in the next chapter we learn to walk in God's ways and not ours. We have power in God when we do it His way. He provides all the provisions along the way for us. You will see God's ways teach us how to unlock doors and open them as well as walk through to the victory, as God guides us and provides for us all along the way.

CHAPTER CONTENTS

CHAPTER ONE

<u>I've Seen Too Much</u>

We had prayer at our church one Friday evening. I remember there wasn't a great turn out of people. But that never bothers me. When I pray by myself or in a group, I always cross over into the spirit and it becomes just me and God. As I began to pray, the Spirit moved on me and I began to shout "I've seen too much" over and over I began to proclaim I've seen too much. This really got into my spirit. I felt that faith was arising in me and the more I shouted the more faith I felt. You see I've seen God do through me so many miracles that the more you see and experience the more I can believe for.

Let me take you back to where it all began. I had only been saved for a little while and on a Sunday morning responding to the altar call of the Pastor along with about two hundred others, I was waiting on the Pastor to come my way. I remember it like it was yesterday. He was all the way on the other side of the church praying for people and as I was focused on the Lord; God spoke to me loud and clear. He said I have called you to preach my Word. Now I was a shy and timid person, and that scared me and excited me at the same time. I told the Lord in my spirit that I wouldn't know where to start that He would have to do everything that I couldn't and wouldn't know how to do. At that moment all the way across the room my Pastor, stopping dead in his tracks and shouted back across the room to me and said, "Thus says the Lord you have asked a hard thing but so be it." I was so messed up, I couldn't believe that I was so bad that it would be hard for God to do in me what He wanted me to do. You see sometimes we don't understand what God is saying or we don't have a full understanding. The disciples knew this also in many scriptures the Lord would take them aside and explain to them what He was saying or doing. After a few years of praying and learning I finally got what he was saying. It wasn't too hard for him; it was going to be hard for me. That there would be a lot I would have to learn. And let me tell you the best way to learn is what I call on the job training. Every storm or circumstances we go through is meant to grow you up in faith. You cannot do the big things for God until you learn who He is.

So as the years went by, God was dealing with me and teaching me, one time I remember going to Peru for the first time doing an evangelistic crusade, I was praying in a little village in Peru and this little momma carrying her baby only a couple months old at best. This little baby had a golf ball size tumor over its right eye, as I laid my hands on it, it slowly began to shrink. It took about two hours or more, I couldn't take my hand off. So I kept one hand on the baby and my team would bring people for me to pray for with the other hand, this went on for about two or three hours and that baby's tumor slowly began to go down little by little until it was gone.

When you see things like this it lifts your faith to believe for more. The more you allow God to do through you the more you can believe He will do. As I write this book, I have traveled the world and seen God do so many amazing things, that now it's like I can believe that God can do anything. In fact that's what was happening in the prayer meeting, I was recalling some of the miracles God has done through me and it began to build up my faith until I began to shout I've seen too much, I mean after all I've seen God do so much, so how could you believe there is something He couldn't do. The more God does the more you can believe for.

I remember the time God was moving greatly in my crusade; miracles were happing right and left, as they say. I was rising in faith and getting very bold. Setting in a meeting my eyes connected to a man in the congregation that needed a miracle. As we looked at each other from a distance I began to tell Jesus I want this one. I want this guy healed.

Now I was talking to Jesus in my spirit. And I want to go on record that this is wrong, you don't tell Jesus you listen. But I had to learn a lesson. I didn't even know if he needed a miracle, but faith was rising in me and I was getting bold. The lesson God taught me I will never forget. When I called the altar call many came forward. The altar was full, as I went down the line praying for people and they were being touched and many healings took place, but I was about to learn a lesson from God that would change my life forever.

About halfway through, there he was. The man that I asked for, the one I told God, that one, that's the one I want God. There he stood right before me. As I asked what he needed from God I found out that he could not hear or speak as he was deaf and dumb, and if that wasn't a big enough shock right beside him were two men with the same problem and the one that I asked for was staring me right in the face. I remember praying and laying hands on them. You could see the one that I asked for wanted it so bad, he began to cry. The more he cried the more I prayed. The other two got it and received their miracle and were rejoicing with laughter. This made the one even more excited and desperate, crying even more, but nothing was happening. After a long time praying for him he finally went back to his seat disappointed. I remember after so many miracles people getting saved, healed, this one, that didn't get it, that one that I wanted seem to take away from all those other miracles.

Going back to my hotel room I began asking God why. I have learned not to ask God the why question too much, just trust him, but this one really messed me up. So, I cried out to Him. Boy did he ever answer me. You know I had begun to think it was me. That God would do what I wanted, but I was there to do what He wanted. God said it was Him that was asking me to do these things, not me telling God. It was Him doing the miracles that I should not ever lose sight of that. I never got back to that church and can only hope God healed that man, because after all I take responsibility for my actions. I will tell you this; I will never lose sight of who is in charge again.

As you begin to see God do these kinds of things through you, the more you see the more you can believe for. That's what I mean when I received that revelation. I have seen too much to not believe. When you have seen this kind of power you begin to expect more. It's not that you just believe. You moved beyond that, now you expect to see more. And if it doesn't you begin to ask why. This is what I was saying to God. I've seen too much, in other words I know you will do more because I've seen you do too much to stop now, I have the faith to move mountains, because after all

I've seen too much already. It's like we are saying:
The sky is the limit.

CHAPTER TWO

<u>The Sky is the Limit</u>

In this Chapter I'm using the term the sky is the limit. Let me explain what I'm talking about. I know this is a very common term in today's society. But this is a term I use in prayer a lot, expressing to God that the only limits I see on me, my ministry, my family or anything else, are the limits that are in heaven and I know you're thinking there are no limits in heaven, right! Well hang on to your hat as we dive into this. First let me set the stage with a verse from the Bible.

Matthew 6:9-10

9 After this manner therefore pray ye: Our Father which art in heaven, Hallowed be thy name.

10 Thy kingdom come, Thy will be done in earth, as it is in heaven.

What this verse is saying, is to speak this or call this, its saying this is the way our lives are to be here and now. So, let's look at how heaven is, this way we will know what to look for and how to live.

First off, I want to tell you that heaven is a real place not a state of mind or condition, it's an actual place. The Apostle John speaks of heaven as the Holy City.

Revelation 21:12

And had a wall great and high, and had twelve gates, and at the gates twelve angels, and names written thereon, which are the names of the twelve tribes of the children of Israel:

John 14:2-3

2 In my Father's house are many mansions: if it were not so, I would have told you. I go to prepare a place for you.

3 And if I go and prepare a place for you, I will come again, and receive you unto myself; that where I am, there ye may be also.

As we see in these verses heaven which is referred to as she has large walls around it and in John 14 there are many mansions, which by the way are for you and I, this shows us a picture of what heaven is going to be like.

There is also Joy in heaven, unspeakable joy:

Psalm 16:11

Thou wilt shew me the path of life: in thy presence is fulness of joy; at thy right hand there are pleasures for evermore.

Isaiah 35:10

And the ransomed of the LORD shall return, and come to Zion with songs and everlasting joy upon their heads: they shall obtain joy and gladness, and sorrow and sighing shall flee away.

Wow, we will have joy, unspeakable joy. In His presence we have joy. Laughter will flow out of our mouths and our mouths will be singing. I'm getting happy, just thinking about this.

I remember one year when we went to Peru, we traveled to a remote area village for a two-day meeting. The little hotel we slept in wasn't much, but the hunger for God was real. However, there was something different in the atmosphere, you could sense it. We arrived in the church for the morning meeting. It was pretty much a normal type meeting with a small crowd. It was a time for the people to get to know who I was. My interpreter Ivy who accompanied us on our trips, she spoke their language and she had one of those personalities that people just love. So, it didn't take too long that they were warmed up and were ready for God. I spoke, and God showed up, and we had an awesome meeting. Now we, break for lunch and some alone time before the night meeting, I had no idea what was about to happen, but take my word for it, God really does want us to live like it's going to be in heaven here on earth and the sky is the limit. I mean we walk around with the weight of this world and all its problems when God wants us to be happy and full of Joy.

That night the word had spread, and the place was packed out and God began to show up and show off in the service. I mean miracles were happening, we had people being healed from back pain and leg pain, but then God started opening blind eyes, I don't remember the exact number, but it was more than 10. But I noticed the people weren't excited. I mean some of them just got their eye site back and they weren't even smiling. For a lack of better words, they looked normal, like it was just another day. I thought to myself, come on, God just healed you and it's just another day. I got off in the corner and began to ask God what's going on, after all I was so excited for them, that I was ready to take off running. God told me there was a curse on them, so I began to pray and break curses off of them and they began to break loose and for the first time since I had been, there they began to smile, and laughter filled the house.

We had a team of 7 people in that place. God had me touch the finger of one young man who was with us named Daryl. I know this may sound crazy, but it was index finger to index finger like the ET thing. And God told me to load his finger, people you can't make this stuff up. So I did what God asked and boy oh boy. Daryl began going around touching people with that finger and everyone he touched would break out in uncontrollable laughter like I have never seen. There were people rolling on the floor, laughter everywhere. People began to sing and dance, they laughed and sang and danced until about 2 or 3 in the morning, you ask why would God do that, because the Bible says the Joy of the Lord is our strength (Nehemiah 8:10) and that's the way it's going to be in heaven so that is the way it should be here on earth. We are to be in His presence here on earth just like when we get to heaven, and when we get in His presence its joy unspeakable.

Also, in heaven sorrow and sighing shall fall away and be replaced by joy and gladness. My friend, it's not only in heaven, that's the way He wants it here on earth for us.

In heaven we will have transformed bodies where there is no more pain. Wow God has provided healing for us right here on earth. Peter said by His stripes we were healed. That means it's already done, past tense. The Bible teaches us that we can walk in divine healing. However, there are many who are sick even though the Bible is clear that by Jesus' stripes (1 Peter 2:24), so why are they still sick? There are many reasons, but one main reason is the same reason that all the world isn't saved, even though Jesus died for their sins! We must reach out and take what Jesus gave us through faith! We as believers are entitled to our healing, but if we don't reach out in faith and accept what was given to us, it won't be manifested in our lives. There isn't one time in the New Testament, where a Christian was sick or diseased and they never received their healing. Jesus even tells us to go out and cast out demons, heal the sick as in:

Matthew 10:8

Heal the sick, cleanse the lepers, raise the dead, cast out devils: freely ye have received, freely give.

The scriptures are very clear that those who believe upon Jesus are automatically entitled to the promises of the new covenant. The Bible doesn't say that, this ends before the return of Christ, and therefore there is no biblical reason to believe that healing is not for today.

CHAPTER THREE

<u>God Started Start</u>

Revelation 22:13

*I am Alpha and Omega, the beginning and the
end, the first and the last.*

He says He is the beginning and the end and not
only that, but the first and last. The Bible teaches
us that God always was and always is. There has
never been a time He wasn't or isn't.

In Jeremiah 29:11

*For I know the thoughts that I think toward you,
saith the Lord, thoughts of peace, and not of evil,
to give you an expected end.*

Okay the Preacher in me is starting to rise up
right here. The Lord thinks about us. Wow is it just
me or do you get that the Lord God almighty
thinks about us. It goes on to say:

Verse 11

Thoughts of peace and not of evil, to give you a future and a hope.

Here He thinks of your life from beginning to end.

Hebrews 12:2

Looking unto Jesus the author and finisher of our faith; who for the joy that was set before him endured the cross, despising the shame, and is set down at the right hand of the throne of God.

You can't get to heaven without faith. Yet Jesus is called the author of Christian faith. Jesus didn't want to go to the cross, it was the Father's will and Jesus was obedient to His Father's will, which is a perfect demonstration of living faith and He refines it and finishes it. That means He knows from beginning to end and he works on us. The Lord pursues us till we get saved. Up until that point He pursues and moves things in our life to get our attention. Once by faith we receive him, then the Bible says:

Jeremiah 29:13

And ye shall seek me, and find me, when ye shall search for me with all your heart.

Now you have received Christ and he says tag you're it. Now we are to search or seek Him. He is not in our past, He's not in our now, He is in our future saying come on keep searching, keep seeking. The Holy Spirit leads us, keep running after and following Him. He is the author and finisher. He's up there at your end looking back to your now and saying come on you got this, take another step, good job now come on take another step. Don't stop, don't stop. I hope you understand that Jesus loves you so much that He went to the cross even when He didn't want to, just because He loves you so much. You came from heaven and He has a plan for us. So He started us before we were born and He finished us before He started us. So, He started start and even finished before He started start. Come on now, this is why you have the victory. God began a good work in you, and He finished it before we even started, all we got to do is follow him He's got this. You could say this before the world began. Genesis chapter 1 verse 1 saying in the beginning and Revelation at the end He started it and finished it even before it began; this is why you have the victory even before you start. Start in Christ and you finish in Christ you have the victory in Christ.

CHAPTER FOUR

<u>In Christ We Have Victory</u>

1 Corinthians 15:57

But thanks be to God, which giveth us the victory through our Lord Jesus Christ.

Our victory is Jesus, amen. So, if you're saved you have victory living inside you. This is why, you don't fight for victory you already have victory. So, we should fight from a position of victory. This changes the game if you go into a battle knowing you have victory even before you start. The Bible teaches us that we are victorious. In the last chapter we found out that God started start and finished it before He started it. Now I want to show you that you are victorious even before you start into a battle. If you go into a fight knowing you have already won that should make it easier to fight. In fact, we will see that God says we are victorious 100% of the time. So, we should be victorious 100% of the time. This doesn't mean we don't fight; it means that we win, all the time.

Colossians 3:1-5

1 If ye then be risen with Christ, seek those things which are above, where Christ sitteth on the right hand of God.

2 Set your affection on things above, not on things on the earth.

3 For ye are dead, and your life is hid with Christ in God.

4 When Christ, who is our life, shall appear, then shall ye also appear with him in glory.

5 Mortify therefore your members which are upon the earth; fornication, uncleanness, inordinate affection, evil concupiscence, and covetousness, which is idolatry:

If we are raised with Christ we rise in victory, victory over the enemy. We don't fight things. The Bible says we are seated with Christ in heaven, so what does that mean with Christ? It's your identity in Christ.

This is where you go ahead and SHOUT because you have victory.

Psalm 23:4

Yea, though I walk through the valley of the shadow of death, I will fear no evil: for thou art with me; thy rod and thy staff they comfort me.

Look again at this verse it says we go through, not live there. Life is a combination of valleys and mountains. The defeats and victories, failures and successes; however, in the times of the valleys where the battles are fought you develop character. This is the God like character. Sometimes in the shadowy valleys you can't see your destiny, but God will never leave you, it says fear no evil, so even in these times of dark places God sees and directs, even when we don't see. Sometimes life's valleys are unavoidable.

John 16:33

These things I have spoken unto you, that in me ye might have peace. In the world ye shall have tribulation: but be of good cheer; I have overcome the world.

In Christ we are overcomers, or you could say victorious. Every time you are on the mountain, you're looking at the valley. The valley is where you fight but remember you're already victorious. My God, this changes everything. We win before we start. So now if you're in the valley you're looking at the mountain top. The mountain top is where we worship and praise God (draw close to God). It's time to dance in the victory. So, if you are on the mountain, you're looking at the battle (valley) and if you're in the valley you're looking at the victory (the mountain). No one is exempt from battles in life. Good people, bad people and all people. But if you're saved if you're in Christ you have the victory. My God I'm about to shout. Remember also there is a beginning and middle and an end to the shadows of death or valleys, they are seasonal.

1 Peter 1:6

Wherein ye greatly rejoice, though now for a season, if need be, ye are in heaviness through manifold temptations:

Say what? It says a little while. It's not eternal. You walk through the valleys. They have a beginning at some point you will come down off the mountain and fight in the valley. There will be a time then it will come to an end. At which time you go up the mountain to celebrate victory. Remember valleys have purpose, it develops a God like character in you and you develop faith in God. You don't have to worry, not only do you have victory, but God will make sure you get back to the mountain top. It says your rod and your staff comforts me. Listen refuse to be discouraged. He is with you, even if you can't see him or see where you're going, he can and he will never leave you. Plus, he says you have victory in him. Before we move on, if you look at the rod and staff, we see staff is for direction. The Shepherd used the staff on the sheep to keep them from wondering off by gently nudging them in the direction he wanted them to go. While the rod was used for protection; now he used it to protect the sheep by striking other animals that are a danger to his sheep. Our Lord does this for us in the spirit.

Last thing I want to look at in this verse is the shadows. We've talked about the valleys, but it says the shadows of the valley of death. Shadows make me think of dark, in darkness we don't see very well. Even if your path is not very clear remember God started start and finished it before He started it. So, he knows where you are and where you're going at all times. Shadows always appear bigger than they really are and that's what's happening here. It tells us they look bigger than they really are, why because God is with us and he says we have already won. We have the victory. Next, I want you to see is shadows can't hurt you. If we stay in Christ and in faith we might go through some stuff, but we win. In Christ we have power over the devil. Now are you ready for this, in order to have a shadow there must be light, oh come on now. Jesus said he will never leave you. If you're in Christ, he is with you and he is light.

2 Corinthians 5:17

Therefore if any man be in Christ, he is a new creature: old things are passed away; behold, all things are become new.

Your old man or old nature is dead. You could say the way you used to think. We now have a new way of thinking. We have the mind of Christ. Know who you are. You are in Christ, you are victorious. You have authority in Christ. You have His name, the name is Jesus, which is above all names even sickness and disease. Come on the Bible says that the earth is the Lord's and the fullness there of.

We need to know who we are and whose we are.

Matthew 3:10-12

10 And now also the axe is laid unto the root of the trees: therefore every tree which bringeth not forth good fruit is hewn down, and cast into the fire.

11 I indeed baptize you with water unto repentance. But he that cometh after me is mightier than I, whose shoes I am not worthy to bear: he shall baptize you with the Holy Ghost, and with fire:

12 Whose fan is in his hand, and he will thoroughly purge his floor, and gather his wheat into the garner; but he will burn up the chaff with unquenchable fire.

What we need to know is: are we the wheat or are we the chaff? Are we baptized with Holy Ghost and fire, or the unquenchable fire?

The way they would make bread is to take the stalk with a fork and throw it in the air. The chaff would blow off and the wheat would come back to the ground.

Then they would crush the wheat to powder. Spiritually this is what he's talking about. As we are thrown into the air and the chaff, our circumstances are blown away.

God takes his Holy Ghost fan and brings change into our lives. When we come back down to the ground we are wheat.

You are a new creation, you are victorious, and you are a winner, not sometimes but all the time. The only thing is you must be in Christ, which makes you a new creation.

CHAPTER FIVE

<u>We Have Authority for Victory</u>

Matthew 8:8-13

8 The centurion answered and said, Lord, I am not worthy that thou shouldest come under my roof: but speak the word only, and my servant shall be healed.

9 For I am a man under authority, having soldiers under me: and I say to this man, Go, and he goeth; and to another, Come, and he cometh; and to my servant, Do this, and he doeth it.

10 When Jesus heard it, he marvelled, and said to them that followed, Verily I say unto you, I have not found so great faith, no, not in Israel.

11 And I say unto you, That many shall come from the east and west, and shall sit down with Abraham, and Isaac, and Jacob, in the kingdom of heaven.

12 But the children of the kingdom shall be cast out into outer darkness: there shall be weeping and gnashing of teeth.

13 And Jesus said unto the centurion, Go thy way; and as thou hast believed, so be it done unto thee. And his servant was healed in the selfsame hour.

Sometimes for a lack of knowledge the enemy can steal our victory, even though it is our God given right as a believer in Christ.

1 Corinthians 15:57

But thanks be to God, which giveth us the victory through our Lord Jesus Christ.

The Word of God is one thing the enemy can't do anything about. It is because the Word of God is God's power.

Romans 1:16
For I am not ashamed of the gospel of Christ: for it is the power of God unto salvation to every one that believeth; to the Jew first, and also to the Greek.

Wow if you believe the Word of God the enemy can't defeat you. But if you don't he can defeat you, it's as simple as that. In the army you have authority over the men that are under you. You also have authority over you and the authority you have for the people under you stops working when you don't obey the authority over you. It's the same way in the Spirit if you obey (believe in the Word) you have authority over the enemy. This is why it doesn't work for so many people. If you don't have and believe in the Word of God, you have no power, and the enemy doesn't have to obey you. Listen you can't just speak the Word you have to believe it. You have proclaimed it in faith.

In Matthew 18 we see the Word of God a seed. And the enemy will always try to steal you seed. For the seed to grow it must be planted in good soil. In other words, we need to not only speak it but believe it in our hearts. In order to do that you must receive it in faith. If you understand it and receive it, then it has power, and the enemy can't touch it. This is why the Bible says the Word cannot return void. Come now Jesus is the Word. Now receive Him, you receive His Word, now believe it and confess it, now you are unstoppable.

CHAPTER SIX

<u>How Do I Open the Door?</u>

We deal with doors every day, doors of opportunity, and doors of breakthrough. Yes, we are talking about spiritual doors. These are doors of opportunity, new territory, doors of break-through, and advancement. Doors are entry points to win victory. However, we still struggle to gain access to everything God has for us, because sometimes we are stuck on the wrong side of the door. The doors seem locked, and we don't know how to open them spiritually.

Matthew 16:13-19

13 When Jesus came into the coasts of Caesarea Philippi, he asked his disciples, saying, Whom do men say that I the Son of man am?

14 And they said, Some say that thou art John the Baptist: some, Elias; and others, Jeremias, or one of the prophets.

15 He saith unto them, But whom say ye that I am?

16 And Simon Peter answered and said, Thou art the Christ, the Son of the living God.

17 And Jesus answered and said unto him, Blessed art thou, Simon Barjona: for flesh and blood hath not revealed it unto thee, but my Father which is in heaven.

18 And I say also unto thee, That thou art Peter, and upon this rock I will build my church; and the gates of hell shall not prevail against it.

19 And I will give unto thee the keys of the kingdom of heaven: and whatsoever thou shalt bind on earth shall be bound in heaven: and whatsoever thou shalt loose on earth shall be loosed in heaven.

Verse 15 is asking, *"Who do you say?"* In other words, it's asking you who do you say He is? First, we need to answer this question before looking at the spiritual doors. Then in verse 19 He gives us the keys. Keys give you access to doors that are closed and locked. Keys remove the barriers between heaven and earth. That's why it says in verse 19, whatever we bind or loose on earth it's bound or loosed in heaven. He gives you the keys which are the power to open doors or close doors and heaven will back you up. However, there are many doors and some open differently. You have to have the right key for the right door. That's why this verse says key(s), like more than one key. This is why some people can't get the doors open. I will talk to you about 3 different doors.

First: Locked doors: These can only be opened by God Himself; these doors people kick and scream, and try to pick the locks, but nothing happens, they remain locked. Later God opens the door at the right time for the right reason and then we see why it wouldn't open for us and we are usually grateful.

Second: Timed doors: God is the Alpha and the Omega, the Beginning and the End. Jeremiah 29:11 tells us He has a plan and a purpose and a future. So, He has your life laid out and knows when to do what. So, at the right time He unlocks the door. It's like the men in the Bible who are waiting on the angel to come and stir the water, the first one in was healed. There was a time for the stirring, and it didn't happen until that right time.

Third: Unlockable doors: These doors take keys, or in today's society, a code or even a pod like we use on our car. He is telling us the door can be unlocked and that's why we were given the keys. Let me list some of the keys that are in the Bible. We have the key for healing which is:

James 5:14

*Is any sick among you? let him call for the elders
of the church; and let them pray over him,
anointing him with oil in the name of the Lord:*

Here is the key, calling the elders together and
praying. It even says confess your sins, but that is
too much, or this is too embarrassing for us.
However, it's the key.

  Then there is forgiveness because the Bible says
to us in:

Matthew 6:15

*But if ye forgive not men their trespasses, neither
will your Father forgive your trespasses.*

  Before forgiveness comes, we must forgive
others. So, the key to forgiveness is unforgiveness
must be dealt with first.

  Now the key that a lot of people really don't like
is the key to provisions. The key here is to give.
Your harvest is always connected to your seed. I
know we don't like this one, but it's true. The key
to prosperity is giving. Let me show you, there are
many verses in the Bible, but I think this one will
show you.

Luke 6:38

Give, and it shall be given unto you; good measure, pressed down, and shaken together, and running over, shall men give into your bosom. For with the same measure that ye mete withal it shall be measured to you again.

Come on this is saying the more you give the more He gives back. You want more then give more. In these last days, the enemy has attacked our families and relationships, well good news, there is a key for that as well.

Ephesians 5:25-26

25 Husbands, love your wives, even as Christ also loved the church, and gave himself for it;

26 That he might sanctify and cleanse it with the washing of water by the word,

I promise if the husbands follow this, they won't have a problem with their wives. And not to be left out wives your key is:

Ephesians 5:22

Wives, submit yourselves unto your own husbands, as unto the Lord.

This is the key to a happy relationship.

  If you are having trouble opening doors (spiritually) you need to look carefully at the keys you're using. There is a key for every promise in the Bible. Remember Satan will try to put doors in your path that will miss direct you. Opening the wrong door can result in curses, sicknesses, even death. Make sure you're using the keys of the Bible. After looking (praying) over the door and know it's God`s door, then go to the book for the right key. Now insert the key, and turn it, if it unlocks open it. Come on you have only one more step. That is to step through the doorway to the other side. Sometimes this will require faith. But the hard part is done. You are a child of God. You do your part, and He will do His.

  Now you've been on the wrong side of the door long enough. Go get those keys and let's walk through to the other side. Once you have found the right key/code and the right door unlocks, open it, now you're looking at what God has for you. Sometimes it easy, just take a step, then again sometimes you're looking at BIG, I mean way over your head BIG. That's okay; God gave you the keys to open it. He wouldn't have allowed that if He didn't want you to go through it or do it. Bible says in Isaiah 43:16 God makes a way. Hebrews 12:2 says He is the authority and finisher of our salvation. Jeremiah 29:11 says he has a plan and purpose, and hope. He will help you; He won't leave you. Now come on get your keys (Bible) and look for the right keys for the right door and unlock it. Now open it, don't be afraid, step through, go ahead God is with you, and it's time.

CHAPTER SEVEN

<u>Your Way or God's Way, Your Choice</u>

Wow we have covered a lot of ground so far. But in order for us to be champions for Christ, I believe first we need to look and see if we are following God`s way and His Word or are we doing what we think is best. God`s way is His Word, but sometimes we do things that aren't really bad, in fact it might even be good. But is it the way or what God wants at this time for you? Let me show you from the Word what I mean.

Proverbs 14:12

There is a way which seemeth right unto a man, but the end thereof are the ways of death.

And

Proverbs 16:25

There is a way that seemeth right unto a man, but the end thereof are the ways of death

When we see this, it's God trying to show us something a little deeper than what we see on the surface. He will use parables, which are word pictures, a story to get across a spiritual message. For instance, the head may signify the beginning or the first. The hand signifies standing beside someone, like at the right of the Father. The feet signify worship or submission where the face may signify standing before someone and the back usually means that which comes after or at the end.

In our scripture it says: *"it's end."* That means if we do it our way instead of God's way, it could end up in death. The Hebrew word for *"its end"* is achariyth and it means back, that which comes after, final consequences. There it is, that's what God is trying to tell us. It's the end that should be our concern. As we look from a human standpoint, we cannot see that which comes after. Now I know sometimes we see a little down the road called life, but we can't see the final consequences of a matter. We can't see the end. We are subject to time, so we have to wait for time revealed. This is where we need to see it God's way. He lives outside of time and can see the beginning and the middle as well as the end. God sees the whole picture. In God's eyes the achariyth is always in full view. Let's look at it from a human standpoint. Do you remember going to a Christmas parade when you were a little child? Santa was always at the end, but you couldn't see him till he came by.

One by one they came in view as they passed by, you would lean out to see more, but no matter what, you couldn't see the end until it came into view.

God always sees all. It would be like if we could go up in a helicopter over this same parade, we could then see it all. That's God`s view of our life, He see all. He sees the beginning and the end, the achariyth. What he is saying is to consider the achariyth in everything you do. What are the consequences? This is why we are to always seek God first in everything we do, because He knows the achariyth which is the end and when we seek Him first, He will reveal the achariyth to us. He tells us to give our tithes and offerings and he will open up the windows of heaven and pour out a blessing we can't contain. Remember He is concerned with the achariyth; He wants to open the treasure chest of heaven for us. We look at the tithes and offering, but He says it's about the achariyth or the end. You can see this through the whole Bible. The Bible says the wages of sin is death. Again, He's showing us the end results. He's saying always look at the achariyth it's not always about the beginning, He wants you look at the end of the consequences.

Proverbs 19:20

Hear counsel, and receive instruction, that thou mayest be wise in thy latter end.

He is always looking at the end. This is why Satan is so successful. He shows us pleasure for the moment. The Bible says sin is fun for a season. Satan will show you the beginning and even the middle, but never the end. He doesn't want you to see the achariyth, just the fun part. As far as our human nature, we are focused on the here and now. God says it's not always about the here and now, but what about the end, what are the consequences of the achariyth? Always pray before everything and aloud for God to direct us, because He sees all, amen.

CHAPTER EIGHT

<u>There is Power in Your Shout</u>

There is power in your shout, not just any shout, but a shout of faith. In today's Christian circles we shout by sight. When something happens that is good, when we see it we get excited and shout. And that's great, we should shout at the blessings of our God. But I'm talking about a shout that's by faith which will change your situation that you're in right now. That takes a shout of faith to shout when you don't see anything going on. Come on did you bring your shout today? Things are not good for me; I need God in a big way. My friend that's what I'm talking about, it's time for you to shout with faith, that's where the power is. Go ahead give it a try.

Proverbs 18:21

Death and life are in the power of the tongue: and they that love it shall eat the fruit thereof.

Are you ready to start eating the good fruit? The Book of James says blessing and cursing flow from the same mouth. This tells us it's our choice to make. In today's society we speak death or curses, and we speak what is wrong, or bad, we speak the problem, however God is saying no, no, no speak what you don't see. Speak my Word, it's the truth, not what you see or feel. If we learn this, our shout will make a big difference. It is because God is pleased with our faith. So go ahead and shout some more. Do it in faith. We read this in the Bible, in Jericho was a barrier between the Promise Land and where they were. The walls were big and high for protection. The Word says no one in and no one out. These people lived in fear. They had heard about God, He parted the waters; and led the Jews through the wilderness, with the cloud by day and the fire by night. Now He was on their walls. They had become prisoners in their own city. Much like some of us; we allow sin to wall us in and then we have no freedom.

Psalm 27:6

And now shall mine head be lifted up above mine enemies round about me: therefore will I offer in his tabernacle sacrifices of joy; I will sing, yea, I will sing praises unto the LORD.

This says when you are surrounded by the enemy lift up your head. The word 'sacrifices' here means: Shout. Shout for joy. You say how can I shout when the enemy is all around me. That's where the power is. Shout praises by faith. And just like the walls of Jericho, your walls will fall down. It's time to shout the walls down, that is stopping us from the Lord's promises.

In the story of Blind Bartimaeus in Mark 10; Bartimaeus had power in his shout.

Mark 10:49

And Jesus stood still, and commanded him to be called. And they call the blind man, saying unto him, Be of good comfort, rise; he calleth thee.

His shout got Jesus' attention, it stopped Jesus in His tracks. That's power.
Look at verse 47

And when he heard that it was Jesus of Nazareth, he began to cry out And said Jesus "Son of David have mercy on me!"

He heard Jesus was coming by and began to shout. Remember he couldn't see he only heard. He had never seen Jesus before or His miracles. He walked by faith not by sight. In verse 48 they tried to shut him up, but he got louder. He heard, we need to hear and shout. I get so excited over His Word that I shout. When the enemy tries to shut you up it means you're on the right track, shout louder. Don't let the enemy steal your praises.

46

Verse 50

And throwing aside his garment, he rose and came to Jesus.

There is power in your shout. He stopped Jesus in his tracks and called him over. They went to get him, and he threw off his coat. This is not just a coat, but it's a special coat that blind people wore like a cane is today. It let people know that they were blind. He had faith because he threw it off not knowing if he could find it if he didn't get his miracle. His faith stopped Jesus, got his attention, and then by faith he took off the old to receive the new, his miracle. He heard, he believed, and he acted by faith, he stepped out and received. Somebody needs to shout right about now!

CHAPTER NINE

<u>Sound Proceeds Victory</u>

We learned in the last chapter that your shout has power. Here you see that sound or praise has victory. So, if you lose your sound, your shout you could lose your victory.

Psalm 22:3

But thou art holy, O thou that inhabitest the praises of Israel.

Praises send God in first. When you praise God rides in on those praises before us. Come on now that will preach. So, if you want to be victorious, make some noise. Praise Him. Sound victorious before you are. Your sound or shout should not resemble your situation. Your situation should line up with your shout or your sound. Your level of victory is linked to your sound. We wait on God to touch things; He is waiting on us to speak things.

Romans 4:17

(As it is written, I have made thee a father of many nations,) before him whom he believed, even God, who quickeneth the dead, and calleth those things which be not as though they were.

In another words, He is saying make some noise. Your sound can't be tied to what you see, but what's in Christ. Paul and Silas were thrown into jail, and they had no reason to sing. They where falsely accused, they where arrested, they where beaten, and they where in chains. This doesn't say, oh joy, let's sing. But their sound wasn't tied to their sight. It was tied to the Spirit. Listen, you might be in a midnight hour situation right now. Maybe you're saying, if something doesn't happen soon, I don't know what I'm going to do. If you're sound is tied to your situation, you are most likely going to stumble through that midnight hour in silence. Your sound will either keep you in prison or set you free.

Zechariah 4:6

Then he answered and spake unto me, saying, This is the word of the LORD unto Zerubbabel, saying, Not by might, nor by power, but by my spirit, saith the LORD of

We can't let what's wrong with us keep us from worshipping what's right about God. Some of you have tied your sound to your sight; you will find yourself in midnight hour circumstances. It's because your sound has dried up. Your praise has dried up. But let me tell you that your most powerful sound will come in your darkest hour of midnight.

CHAPTER TEN

<u>You Can't Touch This</u>

Once we learn whose we are and what we have, it makes the fighting, the battles easier for us. I mean God saved us and equipped us with everything we need. We win even before we start. That's why the devil fights so hard to discourage us; it is so we don't believe in whose we are and what we have at our disposal.

John 17:16

They are not of the world, even as I am not of the world.

Wow this is just like being an Ambassador from a foreign country, in fact that's what we are, we are from heaven, and that's where our citizenship is.

Philippians 3:20

For our conversation is in heaven; from whence also we look for the Saviour, the Lord Jesus Christ:

An Ambassador is a high-ranking diplomat representing one nation to another; they have diplomatic immunity and safety. This is us as Christians, saved, born again from above. We are washed in the blood of Jesus, cleansed and protected.

2 Corinthians 4:4

In whom the god of this world hath blinded the minds of them which believe not, lest the light of the glorious gospel of Christ, who is the image of God, should shine unto them.

Listen this is saying we are in this world as Ambassadors, but not of this world. We are Kingdom kids, from heaven not bound by Satan or even the natural laws of this world. This is why I title this chapter you can't touch this. Because Satan can't touch us; he has to get us back in this world where we think and act like we are of this world. As long as we are from another world then the other is what we live by, and the other world is heaven. This is not my home; I am only passing through earth till it's time to go home to heaven. This is why Satan works so hard to change your thinking or to keep you from knowing what the Bible says. If Satan can keep your focus on your problems, then you are back in this world. Thinking like a worldly person would be like reaping the results of this world and not heaven.

John 15:5-7

5 I am the vine, ye are the branches: He that abideth in me, and I in him, the same bringeth forth much fruit: for without me ye can do nothing.

6 If a man abide not in me, he is cast forth as a branch, and is withered; and men gather them, and cast them into the fire, and they are burned.

7If ye abide in me, and my words abide in you, ye shall ask what ye will, and it shall be done unto you.

How do we know that His Word abides in you? By what you say, what do you talk about? Is it things of this world, or things of Heaven? I have always said if I can talk to someone for just a few minutes I'll come away knowing about them. Are they heavenly minded or fixed on the things of this world? In John 15 we see three types of branches:

1. Those that abide.

2. Those that don't abide and

3. Those that abide part time.

However, if you don't stay in the vine, connected to the vine you won't produce good fruit. Any branch that stays connected to the vine stays green.

Green wood will not burn and it's hard to break.
However, a piece of wood that is broke off dries
out and becomes brittle, very easy to break and
good for burning. We are ordained and set apart
for this.

John 15:16

*Ye have not chosen me, but I have chosen you, and
ordained you, that ye should go and bring forth
fruit, and that your fruit should remain: that
whatsoever ye shall ask of the Father in my name,
he may give it you.*

We are to bear fruit, we are anointed, and we are
a success. You say things aren't going this way for
me. The Word of God can not lie. To stay in a
heavenly mind set you must think about heaven.
To abide in Christ means to have a relationship
with Him, in prayer and reading the Bible. Go to
church and be around other believers. Unbelief,
doubt, sin will cast your fruit to the ground. This
would be a great place to stop and pray and ask
God to forgive you and to help you get closer.

CHAPTER ELEVEN

<u>It Was a Set Up All Along</u>

I'm not sure about you, but I feel safe in Jesus. I'm like so many others; we have problems, even spiritual battles from time to time. However, when I'm in His presence I feel safe. In fact, that's what the Bible tells us.

Proverbs 18:10

The name of the LORD is a strong tower: the righteous runneth into it, and is safe.

First, we need to be the righteousness of God and we do this through salvation in Jesus. Our righteousness is like filthy rags, but through the cross we give Jesus our righteousness and He gives us His. That makes me want to shout! But then it tells us we need to run into the presence of God and at that point we are safe. In fact, we don't have to ever leave His presence, just stay there and live. But the truth is for the most part we haven't learned how to do that yet. Life is hard and it requires going and doing and sometimes that gets us into battles and spiritual struggles we didn't ask for. Wonder if I told you that no matter what, Jesus has got your back and has already made provisions even before you get there. Let me show you what I'm talking about.

Exodus 14:1-4 & 17

1 And the LORD spake unto Moses, saying,

2 Speak unto the children of Israel, that they turn and encamp before Pihahiroth, between Migdol and the sea, over against Baalzephon: before it shall ye encamp by the sea.

3 For Pharaoh will say of the children of Israel, They are entangled in the land, the wilderness hath shut them in.

4 And I will harden Pharaoh's heart, that he shall follow after them; and I will be honoured upon Pharaoh, and upon all his host; that the Egyptians may know that I am the LORD. And they did so.

17 And I, behold, I will harden the hearts of the Egyptians, and they shall follow them: and I will get me honour upon Pharaoh, and upon all his host, upon his chariots, and upon his horsemen.

After 400 years of slavery God has delivered them, but he leads them to where their backs are to a mountain and they have no where else to go.

56

They look like they are in trouble. They were stuck
between the Red Sea and the mountain and the
Egyptians. Have you ever received a victory and
before you can even celebrate, you're in trouble
again? Well, that's what we see here with the
Israelites. God led them there. Has God ever led
you to a place or maybe into a situation that didn't
look good? I mean what am I going to do now,
God why would you do this, I don't understand?
With God sometimes, what looks like a dead end is
really a set up. There was a reason God led them to
go between the sea and Mount Migdol. They could
have taken a short cut, but God had a different
purpose in mind. Do you remember in Chapter 6
we talked about the achariyth? This being the end,
well that's what He is looking at here? We are
trying to figure out the now and the why, while
God has the end in mind.

   The name of the mountain is Migdol which
means: tower. If you go back in time towers were a
lookout point. You could go up to their lookout
and see a great distance around. I also found out
that they used some mountains as armories. Inside
these mountains they would stockpile weapons,
and even food. Then they would lead the battle that
way, and as they did, they could run into the
mountain and have a fresh supply of ammunitions
and weapons at the right time when they would be
running low. They would go to the tower for more

power. Come on I like to say it this way. There is *"FIRE POWER IN THE STRONG TOWER"*.

Verse 17: shows us God knew where they would have to battle, and all the provisions were there. He knew then what they would need, and He knows now what we need and has already made the provisions. Sometimes it's not about the easiest and shortest way. He has the achariyth in mind. It just might be a set up to show the enemy who is in charge.

Proverbs 18:10 says Jesus is the strong tower. There is fire power in the strong tower. It's there we find comfort, shelter and power. This is power to defeat the enemy.

CHAPTER TWELVE

<u>Conclusion</u>

I would like to take this time to pray with you. The Bible tells us that in Romans 10:9-10 that if we believe in our hearts and confess with our mouths we will be saved. Let me encourage you that if you haven't ever received Jesus before to please say out loud the following prayer, then email us at this address: aofmin@yahoo.com

Jesus please
Come into my heart
I believe you died on the cross
And rose again.
I want to live for you
I will serve you all the days
Of my life
Thank you in Jesus name
Amen.

ABOUT THE AUTHOR

Bishop Dr. Paul Kammer and his lovely wife Pastor Polly Kammer are ordained through the Church of God ministries out of Cleveland, Tennessee and oversee an evangelistic ministry called: Altars of Fire. AOF has taken us to many places in the world to reach, teach and preach to people everywhere. Our international crusades have taken us to Peru and Columbia where we have seen thousands saved, healed and delivered. After the death of our first spouses God brought us together in marriage as well as in ministry. Together we have traveled and served as Pastor's in the Church of God. Our goal is to take the fire of God to this generation.

For more information about
Bishop Dr. Paul Kammer
Email: aofmin@yahoo.com
Facebook: facebook.com/Dr-Paul Kammer

9 7 9 8 7 1 7 4 8 0 6 4 2